ROMANO-CELTIC ART
IN NORTHUMBRIA

—

BY
R. G. COLLINGWOOD ESQ.,

M.A., F.S.A.

British Library Cataloguing-in-Publication Data
A catalogue record for this book is available from
the British Library

R. G. Collingwood

Robin George Collingwood was born on 22nd February 1889, in Cartmel, England. He was the son of author, artist, and academic, W. G. Collingwood.

Collingwood attended Rugby School before enrolling at University College, Oxford, where he received a congratulatory first class honours for reading Greats. He became a fellow of Pembroke College, Oxford, and remained there for 15 years until he was offered the post of Waynflete Professor of Metaphysical Philosophy at Magdalen College, Oxford. He was greatly influenced by the Italian Idealists Croce, Gentile, and Guido de Ruggiero. Another important influence was his father, a professor of fine art and a student of Ruskin.

Collingwood produced *The Principles of Art* in 1938, outlining the concept of art as being essentially expressions of emotion. He claimed that it was a necessary function of the human mind and considered it an important collaborative activity. He also published other works of philosophy, such as *Speculum Mentis* (1924), *An Essay on Philosophic Method* (1933), *An Essay on Metaphysics* (1940), and many more. In 1940, he published *The First Mate's Log,* an account of a sailing trip he undertook with some of his students in the Mediterranean.

Collingwood died at Coniston, Lancashire on January 1943, after a series of debilitating strokes.

.—*Romano-Celtic Art in Northumbria.* By R. G. COLLINGWOOD, *Esq.*, *M.A., F.S.A.*

IT is a commonplace that before the Romans conquered Britain, its inhabitants had reached a high level of achievement in decorative art, and that one result of the conquest was the destruction of this art and the imposition of an inartistic though materially comfortable culture. With this view I do not propose to quarrel; but in certain ways I think it may with advantage be qualified. My present concern is with one such qualification.

In the general decay of Celtic art which is supposed to have followed upon the Roman conquest, one exception stands out conspicuous. I do not refer to the objects produced by the Castor and other local potteries of Roman Britain. They include pretty and ingenious things, but it would be pedantic to call them works of art. I refer to the well-known series of brooches to which attention has been repeatedly called in this place and elsewhere. First and foremost there is what so great a *virtuoso* as Sir Arthur Evans has called the most fantastically beautiful creation that has come down to us from antiquity[1]—the gilt brooch found in the guard-room at Great Chesters. The Aesica Brooch, as it is generally called, is not an isolated thing. It is, as it were, surrounded by a cloud of witnesses to the artistic competence of the people who produced it. At the moment I need only remind you of two classes of brooch, the so-called trumpet- or harp-brooches, and the S-shaped or dragonesque. The strange beauty which inspired a German archaeologist, when he found a perfectly ordinary specimen of British trumpet-brooch, to call it a product of Africa,[2] has never, I think, failed to impress any one who has studied these objects.

Of all these brooches, none, so far as we know, was made before the Roman conquest of Britain. That is universally admitted. But, it is said, they were made in the least Romanized parts of the country, the north, the west, and even in unconquered Caledonia, to which Sir Arthur Evans ascribes the Aesica Brooch. It is implied that they are the lineal successors of the pre-Roman Celtic art of Britain, enjoying a last afterglow in the regions as yet unpenetrated by Roman influence.

This is another of the things which require, not so much to be contra-

---

[1] *Archaeologia*, lv, 186.   [2] *Röm. Funde aus Heddernheim*, ii, 40.

dicted, as to be qualified. The Celtic affinities of this art seem to me to have been emphasized at the expense of its Roman affinities, which are in fact, I contend, no less real.

To begin with the Aesica Brooch (pl. xi). Sir Arthur Evans has called attention to the fact that its ornament is like the ornament on objects found in Scot-

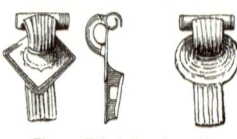

Fig. 1. Thistle-brooches. (½)

land, and is derived from the northern British style of pre-Roman art as we see it at Stanwick. But it does not seem to have been pointed out that the brooch itself, apart from its ornament, has nothing British about it whatever. Sir Arthur did certainly, in the original paper on this brooch to which I and every other student of the subject must

constantly turn with fresh gratitude and admiration, bring it into relation with the brooch worn by a lady on a Roman tombstone at Mainz. But when he wrote, hardly any brooches closely resembling the Aesica Brooch in shape were known. We now possess quite a large number of them, and, as will be shown below, their distribution does not suggest that the Aesica Brooch was a product of Caledonian art.

The Aesica Brooch, as Sir Arthur showed, is derived from the type which German antiquaries call the thistle-brooch (fig. 1). With its humped and reeded bow, its reeded tail like that of a bird, and the disc lying flat on the base of the tail and serving to anchor the foot of the bow to the body of the brooch, this is a remarkably individual and recognizable form; and its dating and distribution are now well established, though the evidence on which the dating is based has mostly come to hand since Sir Arthur's paper was written. It is very common at Roman sites of the early and middle first century in north-western Europe. At Mont Beuvray it appears with a pre-Roman date; but its associations in the Rhineland are not pre-Roman but definitely Roman, and belong to the first half of the first century. In this country it is rare; but when it does occur it is always at places which felt the influence of the Roman invasion at a very early date. Thus we find it at Canterbury, at Lincoln, at Richborough, at South Ferriby, a site remarkable for its large collection of early objects, at Hod Hill, and even in the native village at Cold Kitchen Hill, where a very curious selection of early Roman things has been found. I need not attempt a complete list, but I think it is beyond doubt that wherever we find thistle-brooches in Britain they represent an intrusion of Continental influence in the first years of the Roman occupation. Not a single example has been found which seems to have been in this country before the Romans came, and not a single example which seems to have been in use as late as the Flavian period.

ROMANO-CELTIC ART IN NORTHUMBRIA

The thistle-brooch, then, is a type which belongs not to Britain but to the Continent, and had already passed almost out of use by the time of the Roman conquest. From this type the Aesica Brooch is patently derived. When and where did this derivation take place?

To begin with the when. The Aesica Brooch is not a thistle-brooch, but a fan-tailed type differing from it, though in close relation to it (fig. 2). This

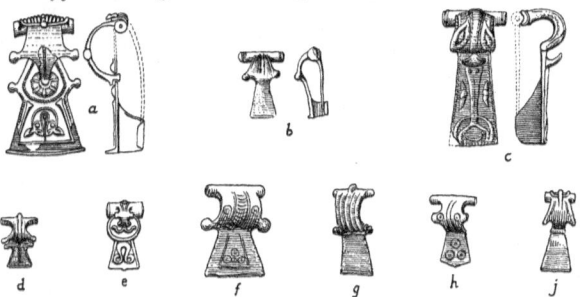

Fig. 2. Bow and fan-tail brooches (½): *a* (Hook Norton), *b* (South Cerney), *c* (Kent), *d* (Woodeaton), *e* (Wroxeter), (Camerton), *g* (Lydney), *h* (Camelon), *j* (Wroxeter).

fan-tailed type recurs at Hook Norton (*P. S. A.* xxiii, 407), at Wylye Camp and at Winterbourne Basset (*W. A. M.* xxxv, 404), at Wroxeter (*Wr.* 1912, no. 3), at Woodeaton (*J. R. S.* vii, p. 114, no. 61), at Canterbury (*Ant. Journ.* iv, 153), at Camerton (*V. C. H. Som.* i, 293), at Lydney (Bledisloe collection), at Camelon in Scotland (*P. S. A. Scot.* xxxv, 403), at South Cerney and Grantchester (Evans Collection, Oxford), and at Santon Downham (*Camb. Arch. Soc.* xiii, 159). Of these examples, only one was found in a deposit of such a kind as to fix the date at which it was in use: namely the Wroxeter example, which dates probably from the early second century. The Canterbury example ought perhaps to be regarded as intermediate between this class and that to which the famous Birdlip brooch belongs.

Let us turn to the Mainz tombstone.[1] This is not itself a dated monument, but Zangemeister thought on epigraphic grounds that it probably belonged to the reign of Trajan. The brooch that appears on this monument is quite clearly not a thistle-brooch, but an example of the related Hook Norton type. As shown in Lindenschmit's plate, it has wings projecting outwards and downwards from the bow; and these wings, which occur at Hook Norton, Camerton, Lydney, South Cerney, Woodeaton, Wroxeter, Camelon, and indeed in almost

[1] Lindenschmit, *Alterthümer unserer heid. Vorzeit*, Band III, Heft ix, Taf. 3.

ROMANO-CELTIC ART IN NORTHUMBRIA

every one of the fan-tail specimens known to me, never appear in the thistle-brooch. Consequently the Mainz evidence of date, such as it is, tallies precisely with that of the Wroxeter example. We must infer that whereas the thistle-brooch belongs to the period from, say, 50 B.C. to about A.D. 50, the fan-tailed type is a derivative of it which flourished about A. D. 100.

The Aesica Brooch obviously belongs to the fan-tailed type. But it is so unusual and unprecedented a thing that we cannot easily say whether it falls early or late in the history of that type. In the development of any type once established, decadence is the general law of art; and so intensely vigorous a work as this, so far removed from anything like the weariness and formalism of a decadent school, can hardly be a late example of its kind. When the history of a type is drawing towards its close, the artist either dully repeats, without conviction and without fervour, patterns which have become mechanical; or else he feels uneasily that this is what he is about to do, and searches for something sensational to relieve the tedium that threatens to engulf him. The Aesica Brooch does neither of these things. Its curves are too energetic to be accused of the one, and too spontaneous, too pure in taste, to be suspected of the other. On stylistic grounds, the Aesica Brooch should be an example of the prototype of which the Wroxeter specimen is a degradation, and this would place the Aesica Brooch hardly later than the Flavian period.

This conclusion, however, is exposed to objection on more than one ground. In the first place, there is one feature about the brooch itself which connects it with a later period. This is the head-plate, the rectangular plate that intervenes between the cylindrical spring-case and the head-loop. This head-plate seems to be a development of the collar which embraces the neck of the head-loop in the ordinary trumpet-brooch; the collar is already beginning to outgrow all bounds in the Backworth brooches, which were found with coins of Antoninus Pius, and it has grown still larger, changing into this plate, both in the Aesica Brooch and in the trumpet-brooch that was found with it. Here, then, seems to be a reason for putting the Aesica Brooch appreciably later than the Backworth type, which belongs to the middle of the second century.

This is a difficulty which I do not wish to minimize. There does seem here to be a certain conflict between a stylistic dating, which would place the Aesica Brooch early in its class, and a typological dating, based on one detail, the head-plate, which would place it the best part of a century later. But at the same time it ought to be pointed out that typological dating has its perils, and that in the present case the perils are acute. The typologist is tempted to think that a more advanced case of a certain tendency must necessarily be later in date than a less advanced. But all he is really entitled to say is that the less advanced type must have begun to appear before the more advanced;

not that every example of the one antedates every example of the other. Now, the more examples we possess, the more nearly we are entitled to the conclusion that typology and chronology coincide; but when we only possess one or two cases of a tendency, the assumption that these can be arranged in a chronological order on purely typological grounds is very hazardous. But this type of exaggerated collar is a thing of which, if I am right, we possess only one example, namely the Backworth[1] (fig. 4, d); and the fact that this pair of brooches was found with coins of the middle second century does not prove that it was not made a good deal earlier. The circumstances of the find are here important. The Backworth brooches were not found in an occupation-level, but in a hoard; and it is the nature of a hoard to be gradually accumulated. The Backworth brooches may have been made in the reign of Pius; but nothing entitles us to assert that they were not made in the reign of Hadrian, or even in that of Trajan. And even if they were made in the reign of Pius, their collar may, for all we know, have been the brother or even the nephew, and not necessarily the father, of the Aesica Brooch's headplate.

I venture then to believe that there is nothing in the typological argument that can warrant us in wholly rejecting the stylistic argument drawn from the comparison of the Aesica Brooch with the others of its class.

There is a second *prima facie* objection to dating the Aesica Brooch before the late second century. It was found 3 ft. above the original floor level, in a guard-room of the south gate at the fort of Great Chesters. The fort was, of course, built in the reign of Hadrian; and from all that we now know about the history of these forts, it is highly probable that the debris in which the brooch was found represents the destruction that took place about 197.[2] That, therefore, is the date at which the brooch was lost. Does not this amount to saying that it belongs to the late second century?

The answer is, once more, that the Aesica Brooch was not in use when it was lost, but hoarded. The evidence of the finders is clear on this point. The two brooches, when they were lost, had been lashed with string to a piece of board for safe keeping or transport (*Arch.* lv, 193). Their position 3 ft. above the floor level suggests that they had been kept in the room over the guard room, and had fallen with the floor of that room when the gate was burnt. In any case, they represent loot in the possession of a soldier, and the date at which he possessed them is not the date at which they were made. The more

---

[1] In a lesser degree it appears elsewhere, e.g. on a brooch (fig. 3 d) of the trumpet type, sub-group R (i), at Traprain Law (*P. S. A. Scot.*, 1915-16, p. 97, fig. 22, no. 1). This brooch might, for all I can see, belong to the late first century.

[2] Until 1929, it was usual to date this destruction *c.* 180 (Dio, lxxi, 7, § 1). Evidence found at Birdoswald in that year seems to demand moving its date to *c.* 197 (*ibid.*, lxxv, 5, § 4). See *Cumb. and West. A. and A. S. Trans.*, N.S., xxx, p. 200; *Arch. Aeliana*, ser. 4, vii, 164.

       G

valuable such things are, the more carefully they are likely to be kept, and the more dangerous it is to assume that the date of their loss must have been soon after the date of their manufacture. On this ground also, then, there is no absolute reason to date the Aesica Brooch late in the second century.

To conclude this part of my inquiry. The evidence of all similar brooches would lead us to put the Aesica Brooch towards the end of the first century or not much later; but in the light of other facts it is not wise to insist on a very early date. I am disposed to compromise and to suggest that it be assigned to the first half of the second century.

Where, then, was this brooch made? Sir Arthur Evans suggested in Scotland, outside the limits of the Roman Empire. That may be right; but the reason he gave was its complete freedom from Roman influences. In the light of evidence that has come to hand since he wrote, I hardly think that this argument can now be maintained. The fan-tailed type to which the Aesica Brooch belongs is not a native type; it is developed from a Roman Continental pattern, the thistle-brooch, and in Britain is limited to the south, with only two exceptions—the Aesica Brooch itself, and the example at Camelon (a Roman fort, not a native site) near the Antonine Wall. The distribution of these fan-tailed brooches is exceedingly difficult to reconcile with the proposed Scottish origin of the Aesica specimen; for, even granting that this specimen stands by itself in many ways, and differs widely in details and in artistic power from the rest of its class, it does nevertheless recognizably fall into that class. Its form is not native but Roman, in the sense that it falls into a class character-istic of the more Romanized parts of Britain, and derived from a type imported into this country by the Romans themselves. It seems, for these reasons, more likely that the Aesica Brooch was made in a part of Britain which had been sufficiently touched by Roman influences to have adopted certain decora-tive motives from the conquerors, and yet remained sufficiently un-Romanized to convert these motives to uses very different from those for which they had been originally employed. In the sequel, we shall see that these conditions were fulfilled in the north of England and the south of Scotland, the land between Humber and Forth, in the first half of the second century. At no other time and in no other part were they ever fulfilled in Britain. To this region and this period, then, it seems that the making of the Aesica Brooch must be assigned.

In order to form a just estimate of the civilization to which I here ascribe the Aesica Brooch, it is necessary to examine certain other works of art assign-able to the same region, and, this time, assignable with no possible margin of doubt. Of these, the most interesting are the trumpet-brooches. These can be classified according to two criteria, into four groups. In the first place, the moulding at the waist may run all round the girth of the bow, or only round the front and sides. In the second place, this moulding may be either plain or enriched with an acanthus above and below. Thus we may distinguish four sub-groups based on these two variables. Sub-group R (i)[1] consists of brooches with a plain round moulding, R (ii) of those with a round acanthus moulding, R (iii) of those with a plain half-round moulding, and R (iv) of those with a half-round acanthus moulding. It has often been pointed out that the half-round moulding ought, by the rules of typology, to be later than the round moulding, and in a general way this is so; but it is one of those typological truths which are only half-truths in chronology. The round moulding in these British trumpet-brooches can be traced back to an earlier date than the earliest known half-round mouldings, but the half-round moulding existed earlier still on the Continent in brooches of a very similar type, and for the most part their history in Britain proceeds concurrently.

Typologically, too, the plain moulding should be earlier than the acanthus; but here again the two existed side by side, and the facts, so far as I can make them out, are not capable of being stated in any simple formula. We are all agreed that the trumpet-brooch is derived from the La Tène brooch of the so-called Aylesford type (*Archaeologia*, lv, 182; cf. *B. M. Early Iron Age Guide*, p. 96; Brewis, in *Archaeologia Aeliana*, ser. iii, xxi, 173, &c.). This has a plain waist-moulding, and there is no doubt that the acanthus was added at some point in the line of development leading from the Aylesford prototype to the fully-developed trumpet-brooch. Two typological steps seem to be distinguishable on this path. First, there is a type which roughly resembles the true trumpet-brooch, but has a straight cylindrical leg and a head bent very sharply over, giving its profile a clumsy and ugly appearance. This profile is like that of the Aylesford brooch, but heavier; and it is rather like a series of ugly little brooches which are the continental derivatives of the Aylesford type. Secondly, there is a group of brooches much resembling these, but differing from them in that their profile has acquired a graceful curve, obtained by giving the leg a convex or concave outline, and not bending the head over so sharply as before. This group is the immediate ancestor of the fully-developed trumpet-brooch, which differs from it only in adding an acanthus on either side of its central moulding.

These two classes of brooch, which I place together as sub-group R (i), (fig. 3), seem to provide the steps by which the Aylesford type develops into the trumpet type. What separates these two steps is the discovery that the ugly profile produced by a straight leg and sharply bent-over head can be greatly

---

[1] In using the letter R for the entire group of trumpet-brooches, I am anticipating the classification of brooches in a work on the *Archaeology of Roman Britain*, shortly to be published.

improved by thinking of the brooch as a single curve, somewhat pear-shaped in outline. When this variety has been reached, we are almost at the true trumpet-brooch; nothing is lacking except the acanthus.

Sub-group R (i), as a whole, is purely British, so far as I know, and the history of it seems to fall in the late first century A. D. The examples of it are by no means common; but when they are put together, they are seen to occur

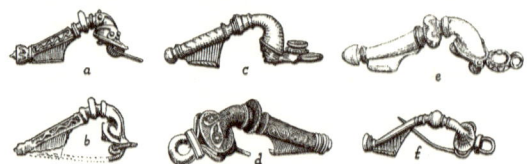

Fig. 3.   Trumpet-brooches, R (i) (⅔): *a* (Segontium), *b* (Forden), *c* (Wroxeter), *d* (Traprain), 'stumpy' variety ; *e* (Deepdale cave), *f* (Newstead I), 'graceful' variety.

at places where there was certainly or probably a Flavian occupation. Thus, we find one at Corbridge (*P.S.A.*, xxiii, 488), one at York (Yorkshire Museum, unpublished), one at Aldborough (Smith, *Rel. Isur.*, pl. xxv, fig. 9), one (fig. 3, *c*) at Wroxeter (*1912 Report*, no. 6, in a stratum of the middle second century, which does not exclude the possibility of its having been in use earlier than that), one (fig. 3, *a*) at Segontium (Wheeler, *Segontium*, fig. 54), of which there is an exact duplicate, from Wroxeter, in the Ashmolean Museum at Oxford (unpublished), one (fig. 3, *b*) at the Forden Gaer (*Arch. Cambr.*, lxxxiv, p. 112), one (fig. 3, *f*) at Newstead in the ditch of the early fort (Curle, *Rom. Frontier Post*, pl. lxxxv, fig. 8), and others at the native sites of Traprain Law (fig. 3, *d*), Deepdale Cave (two, fig. 3, *e*, and another), Bat House Cave, and King's Scar Cave. All the above sites either certainly or probably had an early Roman or pre-Roman occupation; and in at least one case, at Newstead, the brooch was definitely associated with a Flavian deposit. The presence of this type in so many native sites is noteworthy, as suggesting that the development of this pattern out of the Aylesford type was a native, rather than a Roman, development. As for the distribution, it is as a whole unmistakably northern in the sense that these brooches are absent from the south and south-east, the Romanized district, and found over an area extending from central Wales and Shropshire to the Scottish lowlands.

When we come to distinguish between the two varieties of this sub-group, the stumpy and the graceful, it appears immediately that the latter is a more emphatically northern type than the former. The only examples of it known to me are at York, Aldborough, Deepdale Cave, Corbridge, and Newstead. The stumpy variety, on the other hand, is less common in this region, and extends, as we have seen, as far south as Wroxeter and Forden. It may be inferred that the problem of changing the stumpy profile into a graceful one with a single flowing curve was solved somewhere between the Humber and the Forth in the Flavian period.

Sub-group R (ii) (fig. 4) consists of this North British Flavian brooch, altered in one way only—by the addition of an acanthus on either side of the

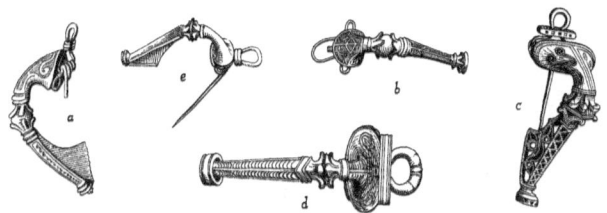

Fig. 4. Trumpet-brooches, R (ii) (½) : a (Newstead), b (Bonsall), c (Risingham), enamelled ; d (Backworth), engraved ; e (Newstead), plain.

central moulding. This addition is a logical development of the previous change. First, the awkward division of the brooch into two parts, one exaggeratedly bent and the other rigidly straight, separated by a moulding in the middle which breaks the design in two, was overcome, and a single curve designed which passes unchecked through the central moulding. But this moulding still forms an uncomfortable break in the profile, and something is needed to connect it with the parts on either side of it. The aesthetic problem is identical with that of leading the eye from the shaft of a column to the abacus on the top of it. A middle term, connecting the longitudinal lines of the shaft with the cross-lines of the abacus, is found in Roman architecture by the use of various capitals, of which the most decorative consists essentially of an acanthus. The same decorative feature, introduced into the trumpet-brooch, completes its evolution, and it is now at last fully formed.

The date at which this last change took place cannot be exactly determined; but it certainly happened well before 140, and it probably did not happen before 100, perhaps not very much before 120. The *terminus ante quem* is given by the numerous examples of R (ii) found in Germany and convincingly interpreted as having been brought thither about A.D. 143; to these we shall return below. The *terminus post quem* is given by the fact that no brooches of this type have been found in the Trajanic forts in Wales, though imitations of it have (Wheeler, *The Roman Fort at Brecon*, fig. 58, nos. 1-6 ; it is possible that no. 3 may be a genuine northern brooch); and this seems to indicate that during the reign of Trajan the fully-developed trumpet-brooch had already begun to be made in the north, but had not begun to be exported from its home except in insignificant quantities, while imitations of it were already being made elsewhere. It seems, therefore, that the addition of the acanthus took place during the first quarter of the second century. But it was certainly not until later than this that the northern workshops began exporting brooches of this type on a large scale.

I have called the decoration on the central moulding of these brooches an acanthus, for that is what, to me, it appears to be. The suggestion has been made (*B.M., Early Iron Age Guide*, p. 96) that it is a development of the hook or hooks which project from the waist of certain brooches often found on the Continent and not wholly absent from Britain. The Aylesford brooch has a single hook of this kind; a double hook is found on a brooch discovered between Ely and Peterborough (*Arch. Journ.*, v, p. 219). These were probably not made in Britain, but the waist-hook also appears on brooches of British manufacture, such as the famous Birdlip brooch, which is dated in the first half of the first century A.D. (*B.M. Guide, cit.*, p. 121), and one found in Kent and ascribed to about A.D. 100 (fig. 2*j*; *Ant. Journ.*, iv, 153). Another was found near Woodeaton with Flavian relics (*J. R. S.*, vii, p. 111, no. 51). These are the only cases that have come to my notice in which the waist-hook occurs on brooches certainly or almost certainly made in this country. Two of them are beautiful examples of Celtic art, the Birdlip brooch among the most beautiful in existence; and they prove that the waist-hook was in use in Britain at the time when the acanthus brooch was invented.

It does not follow that the acanthus is derived from the waist-hook. In the first place, the acanthus brooch certainly originated in the north, and the waist-hook, so far as we know, never occurs in the north. The southern cultural area in which we find the waist-hook did not, in the first and second centuries A.D., stand in any very close relation with the northern cultural area to which we trace the origin of the acanthus brooch; the fact that a certain motive appears in one of these districts does not prove that it was known in the other.

In the second place, if the acanthus developed out of the waist-hook there ought to be at least one intermediate phase traceable. There is no such phase. We know the history of the acanthus brooch to this extent, that we can point to examples of R (i) which are exactly like typical examples of R (ii) except that they lack the acanthus, and we can date them in the Flavian period. They show no trace whatever of the waist-hook. Nor can we point to any examples of R (ii) in which the acanthus shows signs of having been developed out of a waist-hook. In a few cases the front leaf of the acanthus is exaggerated at the expense of the others into something slightly reminiscent of a waist-hook, but all these cases fall late in the history of R (ii), whereas if the acanthus developed out of the waist-hook they ought to fall early.

It is, no doubt, possible that the waist-hook had some influence on the development of the acanthus brooch. Such a development is always a highly complicated thing, and any new type shows, as it were, Mendelian factors inherited from very various and very remote ancestors. If no earlier Celtic artist had ever enriched the waist of a brooch with a hook, very likely the idea of enriching it with an acanthus would not have occurred to a later one. But, on the evidence before us, it is not legitimate to describe the acanthus pattern on the northern British brooches as a 'development' of the waist-hook.

It can, I think, hardly be doubted that the acanthus was borrowed by the northern brooch-makers from Roman architecture. In the south of England the Romans were putting up large stone buildings in the Flavian period; and acanthus capitals could no doubt be seen at Silchester or Cirencester before the end of the first century. But it was not in that part of Britain that the trumpet-brooch was invented. In the north, on the other hand, the Flavian forts had, so far as we know, no stone buildings, and it is not likely that they contained any examples of the acanthus pattern. But about the end of the first century and the beginning of the second—about the time when, as we have already seen, the fully-developed trumpet-brooch was about to come into existence—stone forts like Gellygaer and Hardknot were beginning to be built, and earth forts were in many places being reconstructed in stone. That this movement affected the north of England is abundantly proved. For our purposes, the most interesting of many examples is the legionary fortress at York, whose rebuilding in stone during 'the first decade or two of the second century' is well established (*J.R.S.*, xv, 192; xviii, 78). These new stone buildings must have brought the acanthus capital into northern Britain, and it was shortly after their erection that we find the northern workshops first producing brooches in which this motive was used. It is hardly too much to infer that the native craftsmen had learnt from the Romans a pattern which solved the decorative problem with which at the moment they were struggling, the problem of making the trumpet-brooch into a thing whose lines should flow gracefully into each other throughout its length.

The trumpet-brooch, like the fan-tailed Aesica brooch, is thus no product of the unaided British imagination, but the fruit of a union between imported Roman ideas and native British workmanship. It arose, no doubt, in the less Romanized part of Britain; but it arose only after the Roman conquest of that region, and only as a result of the stimulus given by classical art, even in a

ROMANO-CELTIC ART IN NORTHUMBRIA

debased and mechanical form, to the British artist's mind. It is a commonplace that what we call Celtic art as a whole had a similar pedigree. It was derived from Greek patterns which reached the Celts of central Europe in the sixth, fifth, and fourth centuries B. C., and were transformed by them into the familiar trumpet and scroll motives of Celtic decoration. If this happened once, why should it not have happened again? The Roman acanthus is no doubt a smaller thing than the Greek palmette, but so is the Romano-British trumpet-brooch a smaller thing than the entire range of Celtic art in central and north-western Europe. In all essentials the two cases seem to be parallel. In neither is it just to give the Celtic mind credit for inventing its decorative motives unaided. In both cases it was the impact of a fully-formed and confident classical art that stimulated the Celtic imagination to its highest flights, flights which, if the Celtic mind could never have achieved them without such aid, a less gifted race could not have achieved even with the stimulus of Greco-Roman art to help it.

We must turn to the other sub-groups of the trumpet type. Group R (iii) (fig. 5) has a plain moulding like that of group R (i), but it only goes round the front and sides of the bow, the back being left plain. This type never appears, so far as I have been able to find, in the north of England or in Scotland, though it is common in the south and occurs as far north as the midlands and Wales. It has no one origin, but is derived from various sources. First (fig. 5, *a–c*), it is connected with a type found on the Continent in the first century A. D., and known as Hofheim type I. Actual examples of the Hofheim type are not found in Britain, but its influence seems to be present in certain south-country brooches. Secondly (fig. 5, *d*), this sub-group is in part a descendant of R (i), simplified and cheapened by interrupting the mouldings where they become invisible from the front. Thirdly, it is sometimes (fig. 5, *e–h*) a cheap south-country imitation of R (ii), with the acanthus left out and the mouldings simplified as before. Until these various alternative derivations have been distinguished it is unwise to offer any opinion about its chronology. Examples derived from the Hofheim type might belong to the middle of the first century; examples derived by simplification from R (i) might be late first or early second century; examples derived from R (ii) by simplification cannot be earlier than the early second century and are probably later than that.

As we go farther south, the imitations of northern trumpet-brooches falling into this class (cf. fig. 6, for southern imitations of R (ii), as well as fig. 5, *e–h*) tend to become not less recognizable for what they are, but more tasteless, un-intelligent, and technically poor. In many cases (e. g. *Rotherley*, pl. xcix, no. 1; Wilsford Down, two examples at Devizes Museum, nos. 325, 326; Hambleden, in *Archaeologia*, lxxi, fig. 27) faint traces of the acanthus are present in the

ROMANO-CELTIC ART IN NORTHUMBRIA

form of a milled knob or a pair of tiny lumps, and the animal-head which in the northern brooches is often done in enamel or relief on the trumpet has been degraded into a few meaningless markings. These imitations may in some

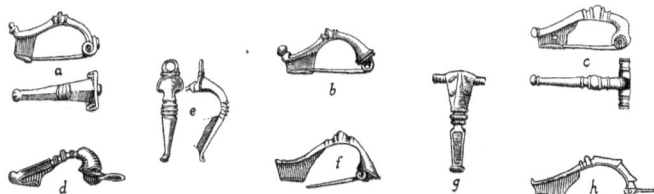

Fig. 5. Trumpet-brooches, R (iii) (½) : *a, b, c* (Reading), continental types ; *d* (Wroxeter, A. D. 110-30), derived from R (i); *e* (Segontium), probably derived from R (ii) ; *f* (Wroxeter), derived from R (ii); *g* (Wilsford Down), *h* (Lowbury), southern derivatives of R (ii).

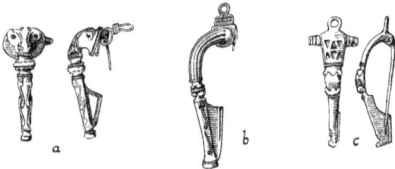

Fig. 6. Southern English imitations of R (ii) (½) : *a* (Cirencester), a typical example of R (i), cf. fig. 1 *a, b*, modified by the addition of an acanthus ; similar examples Lydney, Beckhampton Down ; *b* (Poltross Burn), an import from the south ; similar examples Charterhouse-on-Mendip, Canterbury, and other less close parallels in the south ; *c* (Wooton-under-Edge), a very degraded imitation of a type common in the south-west, the trumpet-brooch assimilated to a well-known southern type.

cases be earlier, but most of them are probably later, than the time in the middle of the century (as I suppose it to be, because of the negative evidence of the Welsh forts evacuated about that time) when the northern workshops increased their production and sent their products all over England, as is shown by examples from Mildenhall (Fox, *Arch. of the Cambridge Region*, pl. xxii), West Stow in Suffolk (Evans Collection), London (Roach Smith, *Illustrations of Roman London*, pl. xxxiii, no. 16) or Tarrant Abbey in Dorset (*Durden Collection*, pl. vii, no. 2), to name a few only. That these southern examples were made in the south no one will believe who considers, first, the enormously larger numbers of the same type found in the north, and, secondly, the exact resemblance between the northern and southern specimens.

Group R (iv), with the half-round acanthus moulding, is fairly common in the north and not rare in the south. Some of the southern specimens (e. g. *Devizes Mus. Cat.*, no. 762, and *W. A. M.*, xliii, p. 180, both from Cold Kitchen

Hill; *Lowbury*, no. 52; *Durden Collection*, pl. vii, no. 3) are obviously of southern manufacture, and probably not earlier than the second half of the second century. In the north, too, this group is inclined to be late, although a fine enamelled specimen from Brough-under-Stainmore, in the Evans Collection, seems to me earlier than 150. It is worth noting that the trumpet-brooches

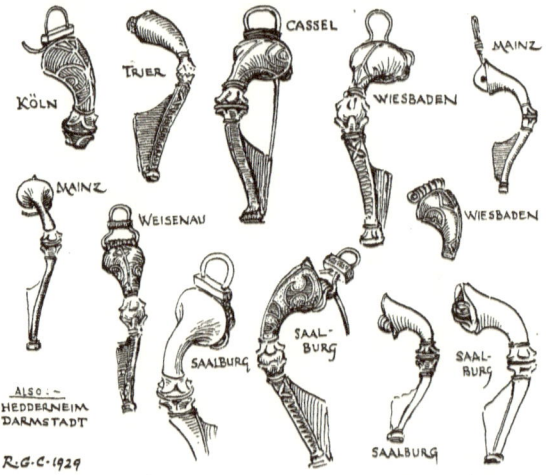

Fig. 7. Rough sketches of trumpet-brooches found in Germany; not local.

found in Germany, to which attention has been called by Dr. Jacobi in *Saalburg-Jahrbuch*, 1912, p. 19, have been connected by him with Professor Fabricius's view (expressed in 'Ein Limesproblem', *Festschrift d. Univ. Freiburg*, 1902) that about the year 143 a large number of Britons were removed from this country as a result of the conquest of the Lowlands by Lollius Urbicus and settled in the frontier district of Upper Germany, where they were employed in constructing the so-called 'outer Limes'. My own examination of the trumpet-brooches in Germany (figs. 7, 8; they have never been published as a group) entirely confirms this suggestion. The brooches in question, so far as I have been able to examine them, are remarkably homogeneous in type, and include nothing which I should ascribe to central or southern England. From the point of view of the student of British brooches they are inexplicable except as representing a sudden movement of people from the north of England

and the south of Scotland ; a movement which took place at one time, about the middle of the second century, and was not repeated. To connect this movement with Antoninus Pius and the Brittones of the Odenwald Limes is a step which no one could refuse to take.

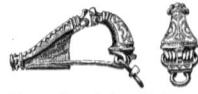

Fig. 8. Brooch from Heddernheim. (½)

It follows that the German examples represent the state of the north British industry about A. D. 140. They include, so far as my observations go, only two ex-amples of R (iv)—one at Heddernheim (fig. 8) and one at Mainz (fig. 7). It is also noteworthy that they include far more enamelled than plain specimens. The inference is that R (iv) did not become common until definitely after 140, and that the enamelled specimens of R (ii) are on the whole earlier than the plain. This confirms the suggestion, made above, that the time when the northern workshops began the 'mass-production' of cheap brooches, to meet a growing demand at a dis-tance, was about the middle of the second century.

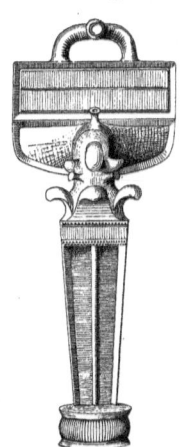

Fig. 9. Trumpet-brooch from
Aesica. (½)

A very large and very ugly example of R (iv) (fig. 9) was found with the Aesica brooch, and shows some instructive features. The treatment of the acan-thus, and indeed the whole design, betrays an over-ripe school of art and shows that the trumpet-brooch has been in existence long enough for people to aim at getting new effects by a sensational exaggeration of its features and an insistence on sheer size. The purchaser was no doubt induced to buy it by being told that it was the largest brooch in the world. The whole style is foreign to that of the German examples, and therefore points to a date definitely later than 140. On stylistic evidence, no more than that can be said. At any time about 150-175 some one might have indulged in an orgy of bad taste with this kind of result. As to its place of origin, a flawed and unfinished casting of a similar brooch, found at Brough-under-Stainmore, is in the Ashmolean Museum (fig. 10). This is the only close parallel, though certain features—notably the exaggerated tray-like head-plate—reappear in a brooch from Cranborne Chase (*Woodcuts*, pl. xiii, no. 10) ; and it is not unlikely that the Aesica trumpet-brooch was made at or near Brough.

If we try to reconstruct the history of the industry after about 140, we soon find ourselves in difficulties. The next stage after that date, as we have

H 2

already seen, is the introduction of cheaper forms and the supplying of a wider market, which seems (since the forms change very little) to have happened quite soon. It probably happened about 150. But what happened next? It is hard to say. We are wholly unable to trace any stages by which the northern

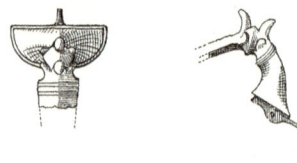

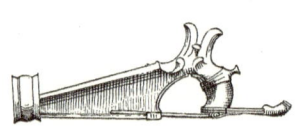

workshops developed or decayed after that time. There are no decadent trumpet-brooches that can be ascribed to the north. The one exception known to me is an exception that proves the rule. This is a really dreadful brooch (fig. 6, *b*) which was lost in the Poltross Burn milecastle before A. D. 197 (*C. & W. Trans.*, N. S. xi, fig. 20, facing p. 440, no. 2). This would point to a catastrophic decline in the art of the northern brooch-makers, but for the fact that others just like it have been found at Charter-

Fig. 10. Above: flawed casting from Brough-under-Stainmore (⅔). Below: trumpet-brooch from Aesica. (¼)

house-on-Mendip (*V. C. H. Som.*, i, 338) and Canterbury (*Collect. Ant.*, vii, pl. xx); and these prove what any one looking at it would suspect, that it is not a northern brooch at all but one of the numerous and, in general, easily recognizable southern imitations. These are, as a rule, confined to the south. I know of no other example found in the north. One is tempted to conjecture that it was brought from the south by a soldier or camp-follower of the Second Legion, when detachments were moved up from Caerleon to garrison Hadrian's Wall while its own auxiliary regiments were on the Antonine Wall between 143 and 197.

There is no evidence that any trumpet-brooches were made in any northern workshops after the end of the second century; and the total lack of developments or debasements referable to the second half of the century (the Aesica trumpet-brooch being rather a freak than either a development or a regular debasement) suggests that the production of this type ceased a good deal before 200—nearer, perhaps, to the middle of the century than to the end. On the whole, the *floruit* of the acanthus brooch, R (ii) and R (iv), seems to have lasted forty or fifty years, from A. D. 110–120 to A. D. 160–170. This dating is, of course, very rough.

A third group belonging to the same time and place consists of brooches shaped like the letter S (fig. 11). These S-shaped or 'dragonesque' brooches have been hardly less admired than the trumpet-brooches; and though they are not in fact so beautiful as these, they are a very fine example of Celtic decorative art. They were not originally dragonesque; that, like the animal-

head on the trumpet-brooches, was an addition to the original design in keeping with the general spirit of Celtic art, which liked to turn things into beasts
whenever opportunity offered.

The earliest form of S-shaped brooch is seen in a little example from
Braughing in the Ashmolean Museum (fig. 11, *a*). It is associated with several

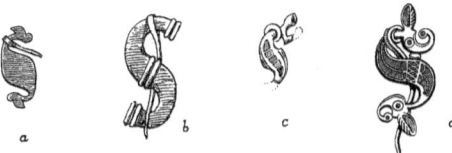

Fig. 11. S-shaped brooches (⅔): *a* (Braughing); *b* (Victoria Cave); *c* (Segontium), beginning to show dragonesque
features, *c.* A. D. 100; *d* (Norton, Yorks.), fully developed dragonesque pattern.

objects dating very little, if at all, later than the Claudian invasion: thistle-
brooches, a brooch of a kind found on Augustan sites on the Continent, and so
forth. It is a simple plate of metal, quite undecorated, with a hooked projec-
tion at either end, one acting as a hinge, the other as a catch. A good deal
later than this are two that show the date at which the dragon begins to
emerge. One, found in the Victoria Cave at Settle, is a clumsy thing with
meaningless mouldings at head and foot and across the middle (fig. 11, *b*); we
have already seen reason to think that some of the brooches contained in these
caves are Flavian, and this may be of the same period. A specimen from
Segontium (Wheeler, *Segontium*, p. 133) is dated about the year 100, and
here we find the head and tail becoming claw-like excrescences, ugly, unpleas-
ing in design, but bearing a little eye-shaped ornament which shows that by
about the year 100 the idea of turning this kind of brooch into a dragon was
already entering the minds of craftsmen (fig. 11, *c*).

It may have been about this time that the decisive step was taken. The
Newstead example shows the dragon fully formed, and dates before the reduc-
tion of the fort in size, that is to say, before 140. It therefore belongs to the
Flavian occupation, or its Trajanic sequel. For the present purpose it is hardly
necessary to reopen the question of the length of this sequel—a question which
can, perhaps, never be precisely answered. At Wroxeter, a very similar brooch
is dated before 130, and these are the only two fully-developed dragon-brooches
which are dated with any approach to accuracy; the numerous examples at
Traprain Law, for example, are so vaguely dated as to be hardly dated at all.

When once the dragon type of S-shaped brooch (fig. 11, *d*) has been established, it seems to banish all the others. At any rate, no S-shaped brooch

that lacks the dragonesque features seems to be necessarily, or even probably, later than about the year 100. Moreover, with very few exceptions, these dragonesque brooches are so much alike that they might be the products of a single workshop. That they did all come from the same workshop I do not suggest; but I do suggest that they were made in the north, where the great majority of them have been found, and represent a brief episode in the history of brooch-making, being perhaps driven from the market by the more practical and more beautiful trumpet-brooch. It is impossible not to be struck by the contrast between the long history and numerous imitations of the trumpet-brooch, and the paucity of varieties and almost complete absence of imitations of the dragonesque. The only imitation known to me is from South Shields.

It seems possible, then, that the S-shaped brooch, after becoming dragonesque and playing a part in the sudden efflorescence of Romano-Celtic art in Northumbria that marked the early second century, disappeared hardly less suddenly about the middle of the century or, more likely, earlier.

A fourth type of brooch that played its part in the same movement was the type which I propose to call the head-stud type (fig. 12). This is a stout, solidly-constructed brooch, its bow bent almost into a semicircle and normally square in section. Along the fore-edge of the bow is generally a band of ornament in enamel; the foot is boldly expanded, and at the head, just below the junction of the bow with the arms, is the stud which forms the most conspicuous feature of the type. The derivation of this brooch from native types of the first century offers a remarkable parallel to the case of the trumpet-brooch. The most striking feature—the acanthus in the one, the head-stud in the other—is in both cases an addition to a first-century brooch that lacked it. This prototype, in the case of the head-stud brooch, is known from the hoard found at Honley, near Huddersfield, and deposited about A. D. 75-80 (fig. 12, *a*). When a head-stud is added to this product of pre-Roman Brigantia, the head-stud type, as I call it, appears.

The date of this appearance cannot be exactly fixed. The *locus classicus* is the Lamberton Moor hoard, found significantly enough near Berwick-on-Tweed and containing what is perhaps one of the finest, and probably among the earliest, examples of the type (fig. 12, *b*). The hoard has been ascribed to the early second century (*P. S. A.* xxii, 59), and as an estimate this can hardly be bettered, but it is not susceptible of proof. Little importance can be attached to the fact that one example has been found in Germany with a coin of Trajan (*Röm. Funde aus Heddernheim*, iv, pl. ix, no. 18); and one from Corbridge, which I should place late in the series, is said (*Arch. Ael.* 3, vii, 40) to 'belong presumably to the middle of the second century', but was found without any associations. An example found at Balmuildy (fig. 12, *c*) must have been in use

ROMANO-CELTIC ART IN NORTHUMBRIA

in the years 140-197, and the same inference may be drawn from specimens on the Wall of Hadrian, and perhaps, though this is by no means clear, at Newstead. One curious fact, to which we shall return, is the presence of several at Traprain (fig. 12, *f*) which lack the decoration on the fore-edge. At other sites, examples with a plain fore-edge seem to be comparatively rare.

That these brooches go back to the Flavian period is very unlikely. They are widely distributed, but none has been found in the pre-Antonine forts in

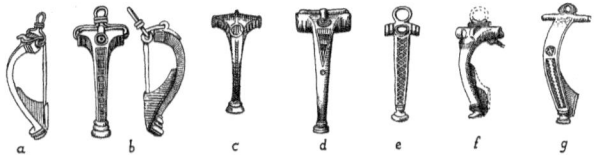

Fig. 12. Head-stud brooches (⅓): *a* (Honley), Flavian; *b* (Lamberton Moor), first half of second century (?); *c* (Balmuildy); *d* (Corbridge), middle of second century (?); *e* (Corbridge), slightly later (?); *f* (Traprain), cheapened form, *c.* 160-200 (?); *g* (Woodeaton), southern imitation.

Wales, and this seems to show that they did not begin to be exported from their home in the north (for there is no doubt of their being originally a northern form) until after the withdrawal of the Welsh garrisons towards the middle of the second century. No importance can, in my opinion, be attached to the fact that one has been found at Trier in the company of a first-century glass vessel, or the fact that their enamel is generally designed in a plain and simple pattern (*Newstead*, p. 323-4). Mr. Curle's view (*ibid.*), that most of them belong to the Antonine period, meaning the years 140-180, is one with which I entirely agree. It seems possible that they began to be made rather later than the trumpet-brooches, and later perhaps also than the dragonesque; but as early as the first half of the second century. In the middle of the century they were very popular, and in the south imitations of them were current which are comparable and perhaps contemporary with the imitations of the trumpet-brooches. An example of what I take to be such an imitation was found in the Caerleon Amphitheatre (no. 12).[1] Others, either continental imitations or very debased products of British worshops, may be seen in several museums on the Continent (Mainz, Trier, Bonn, &c.; fig. 13). They have a hinged pin and no head-loop, and their design is extremely clumsy and far removed from anything that has been found in the north of England or in Scotland.

The history of this group, so far as I can make it out, is that it originated

---

[1] How debased these imitations are may be seen when examples (e.g. *W.A.M.* xliii, p. 181, D; *ibid.*, p. 390, B; or the Woodeaton specimen, fig. 12*g*, at the Ashmolean) are compared with those figured in *e.g.* the Newstead, Traprain, and Corbridge reports.

in the north of England or the south of Scotland, early in the second century, perhaps not before the reign of Hadrian. It was easier to make [1] and to decorate than the trumpet-brooch, and became at least equally popular, being

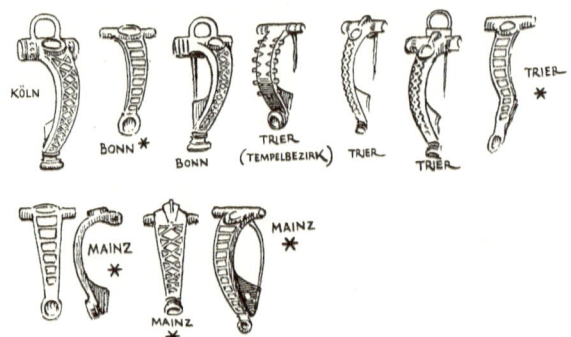

Fig. 13. Rough sketches of head-stud brooches found in Germany (not to scale); those marked * are probably south British or continental imitations of north British brooches.

imitated certainly in the south, and perhaps on the Continent also, in the middle of the century and very likely later. But we do not know what happened to the type in the north, its original home, after the middle of the century. Like the trumpet-brooches, it does not seem to have any history of lingering decline. Its decline falls outside its home district, in the imitations made elsewhere. The only qualification of this statement that can be made applies to the variety without enamel, which may be supposed a late and cheapened form. The fact that this form is common at Traprain Law (fig. 12, *f*), and not elsewhere, is suggestive.

The origin of these four groups of brooches, as our historical analysis has shown, takes us in every case to the early second century, and in two cases out of four yields evidence that the movement which occurred at that time owed its origin to the stimulus of new ideas introduced by the Roman conquest. How far the people who made these things were the successors of the people who made the Stanwick objects I cannot suggest. But it is, I think, clear that however much they owed to the Stanwick school, which was, after all, a school of somewhat effete and formalized decoration, definitely inferior in vigour and taste to its contemporaries in the south, they owed to the new Roman influence

[1] Flawed castings of trumpet-brooches are fairly common at Brough-under-Stainmore; but though head-stud brooches were made there, I have never seen a flawed casting of one.

much of what made their work art instead of mere craft. But before I conclude I must ask how this movement ended.

There is no evidence that it created anything new after the middle of the second century. Indeed, there is clear evidence that it did not. There is nothing strange about that; many movements in the history of art have exhausted their creative energy in a generation and lapsed into mere self-imitation. But the movement whose history we are tracing did not do this. So far from producing mere imitations of its former triumphs, it produced, after the middle of the century, little or nothing. The trumpet-brooch, after 140, did nothing but develop a cheap imitation of itself for mass-production. The head-stud brooch underwent exactly the same process, but its cheap form, instead of being exported in large numbers to the south of England, was very little made except at Traprain Law. Now the head-stud brooch seems to pass through its phases a little later than the trumpet-brooch. Probably, therefore, when the cheap trumpet-brooch was introduced, the cheap head-stud brooch had not yet been invented.

This suggests that the northern British workshops underwent some change, which caused them to stop producing their staple wares, between the general adoption of the cheap trumpet-brooch (? 150) and the introduction of the cheap head-stud brooch, an event which cannot have happened very long afterwards; and that this event did not affect Traprain Law.

What was the nature of this event? We cannot suppose that the northern workshops voluntarily ceased to work, or that they deliberately began to produce goods of a different kind. They were enjoying a regular trade boom, based largely on the cheap trumpet-brooch, and if that boom had continued it is hardly imaginable that they should have abandoned the goods that were being so successful and turned to the production of others. It is far more likely that something happened which crippled their power of production.

If we turn to the historical records of the time it is not difficult to see what this may have been. A well-known passage of Pausanias (viii, 43) tells us that Antoninus Pius annexed the larger part of the territory of the Brigantes because they made an armed attack upon the 'Genounian district'. No one has satisfactorily explained what or where this district was, nor does it greatly matter for my purpose. But the meaning of the emperor's action probably is, as Haverfield pointed out (*P. S. A. Scot.*, xxxviii, 457), that the Brigantes, who before this event were a self-governing *civitas* with a local government of their own seated at Aldborough, were deprived of this home rule in consequence of some unauthorized and violent action, and reduced to a state of dependence on the direct administration of the Roman governor. Haverfield connected this event with the inscriptions recording the governor Julius Verus, who about

ROMANO-CELTIC ART IN NORTHUMBRIA

the year 158 brought large reinforcements to the army of Britain and rebuilt a number of forts as far south as Brough in Derbyshire and as far north as Birrens in Dumfriesshire (*ibid.*).

Thus we have documentary evidence that about the time when the northern British workshops, with the apparent exception of Traprain Law, suffered some kind of disaster that lost them their trade and broke the continuity of their artistic tradition, the men of northern England were punished by Rome for something in the nature of a rising. That this punishment involved more than the mere loss of political rights we know from the fact that Verus re-established garrisons in the Brigantian country. It is possible that the matter did not end there. More than one ruler has felt it necessary to make an example of a people that has risen in revolt after laying down its arms. Julius Caesar, when the Gaulish rebels in Uxellodunum surrendered, 'saw' (in the words of Dr. Rice Holmes) 'that, if these rebellions were to break forth again and again, his work would never be at an end. He was aware ... that his clemency was notorious, and had no fear that any measures which he might be forced to adopt would be misunderstood. He determined, therefore, to inflict upon the garrison a punishment so appalling that all malcontents should in future remain quiet.' It is conceivable that two centuries later another Roman argued in the same way, and carried into the north of England the same methods by which William the Conqueror was to persuade the same region that there was a king in England. If that is what Julius Verus did to the Brigantes, it is not surprising that, except where it lingered out of harm's way in the remote stronghold of Traprain Law, the renaissance of Celtic art that had been produced by the coming of the Romans should have found a sudden end.

Note on the Nomenclature of Brooch-Types.—The provisional adoption, in this paper, of the German name *Distelfibel* for the brooches shown in fig. 1 is open to the objection that the name thistle-brooch is already used for a Viking Age type; the use of the term trumpet-brooch, to the objection that these objects may be thought more like harps than trumpets. Objections of a similar kind can be brought against any nomenclature based on fancied resemblances or places of discovery; and genuinely descriptive names (such as those used in figs. 2, 11, and 12) cannot always be devised. The writer has therefore proposed, in a recent book on *The Archaeology of Roman Britain*, a series of lettered and numbered types for the commoner Romano-British brooches, which, if found acceptable, will enable students to drop these names altogether; but did not feel justified in dropping them in the present paper, which was in type before the publication of the book.

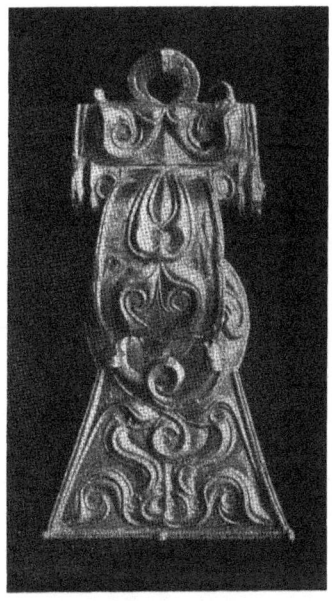

The Aesica Brooch (⅓)

From a photograph by W. Parker Brewis, F.S.A., by
permission of the Society of Antiquaries of Newcastle-
upon-Tyne

www.ingramcontent.com/pod-product-compliance
Lightning Source LLC
Chambersburg PA
CBHW020716180526
45163CB00008B/3107